# HAPPY TIMES

*by*

# LEE RADZIWILL

© text and personal archives 2000 Lee Radziwill

© 2000 Assouline Publishing
601 West 26th Street,
18th floor
New York, NY 10001, USA
www.assouline.com

ISBN: 2 84323 250 3

Printed in Italy

# HAPPY TIMES

*by*

# LEE RADZIWILL

ASSOULINE

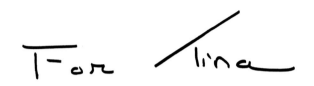

For Nina

# INTRODUCTION

When I look back on my life, it seems nearly everything of interest happened in little more than one decade—dramas, tragedies, major events, pleasures, my close friendships with artists and political figures, the lovely places where I lived in England and New York, the trips to Europe, visits at the White House . . . It seems as if six decades were packed into one. I often wonder how it was possible to absorb so much joy and enthusiasm. I wasn't aware until after it had passed what an extraordinary period it had been. The entire decade.

At the time, I didn't realize how special everything was, although aware certainly that there was magic in the air. Everything seemed exciting, glamorous and carefree. We were presumptuous to assume this magic would continue. There was so much laughter, wit, youth, energy. The possibilities were endless. President Kennedy borrowed a credo from Sophocles, and inspired those around him to try to live their lives along lines of excellence. Everyone wanted to give the most of themselves because that expectation was returned.

That's what Jack brought out in most people, asking for something of particular interest, something original, clever, or different. God, we did have a good time. Maybe that's why it was so brief.

Then the President was killed, and things became flat. Many people couldn't handle his loss; their true colors began to show. The carefree and exciting times vanished. People had to struggle with themselves.

Over a number of years, friends have urged me to write an autobiography. I had the opportunity, but after some thought I decided it would involve me in too many other lives.

I wanted to do something much lighter, which would touch only on the good times. I also felt that so much had already been said about my family and the people I was close to, that it would be more enjoyable to only remember the best times with them.

Happy times were a better choice for me. I am always aware that I've had a special and privileged life, yet it has been balanced by tragedy as it has been for so many others.

I believe that without memories there is no life, and that our memories should be of happy times. That's my choice.

# CONCA

One of the happiest summers was in 1962, when my husband Stas Radziwill and I took the beautiful Villa Episcopio (the house of the bishop) in Ravello, the jewel of the Amalfi coast. It was high on the coast, overlooking the entire Gulf of Naples and Salerno.

Our children, Anthony and Tina, were with us, as well as friends from London. My sister Jackie came to visit with Caroline, who was four years old. The only drawback was the Secret Service, who created an upheaval with their wiring and telephone systems before their arrival; but as the years passed, I got used to that.

Otherwise, life was carefree, with no set hours for lunch or dinner except that they were very late. Only a vague rhythm existed, of waking to hear the fishermen below calling to one another, the hum of the motorboats in the distance, then the shutters opening over an endless stretch of sea.

When everyone had gathered to descend the somewhat terrifying road to Amalfi, my favorite part of the day began.

We took a boat from Amalfi to Conca, an ancient, enchanted fishing village between Amalfi and Positano. The village consists of one long, narrow, winding street leading down to the sea, where a few fishing boats are pulled up on the beach. The houses have terraces covered with oleander and bougainvillaea. It has never changed. Its secret is its simplicity. However, one needs an untiring heart and legs of iron to mount and descend the three hundred and some steps. After arriving at Conca, we would swim endlessly and explore the secret grottos that only a few Amalfians, like our close friend Sandro D'Urso, knew about. Sandro, better known as Papa D'Urso, was our real leader. He would show us how to take the sea urchins from the rocks underwater so their spikes wouldn't cut into our fingers, and how to open them and eat their mustard-colored filling. They are supposed to be tremendously healthy, and are full of iodine—an acquired taste.

After hours of swimming and discovery, we would have lunch at about three or four—incomparable spaghetti made by Rosa (our wonderful cook from the village), followed by some bursting peaches warm from the sun, lots of wine and much laughter.

The path to the sea was overhung by trees laden with lemons and lined with verbena, jasmine, plumbago and clumps of artemesia: a pure paradise.

After spaghetti, we would all take a siesta. Before embarking on our return to Ravello, we would indulge in the ritual observation of life on the piazza in Amalfi for a few hours, while we read yesterday's newspapers over espresso or *gelato*. Later, we would often shop for something: a pair of sandals, yet another T-shirt, an essential *pareo*. Leisurely shopping is an integral part of the late afternoon and early evening in this part of the world.

Finally, early in the evening, we would wind our way up the tortuous curves to Ravello accompanied by the friendly sounds of the tourist buses descending. Then a leisurely bath or shower upon reaching Episcopio, and dinner around ten on the terrace overlooking Amalfi and the lights of the coast. Sometimes we would sail to Capri for dinner on the Agnelli's sailboat, *The Agneta*, recognizable in the distance because of her brown sails. Coming back, we would sing songs like "Volare" ("Nel Blu Dipinto Di Blu . . ."), a charming, senseless song, incredibly popular at the time.

Many saints' days were celebrated with fireworks booming from Amalfi all up the coast to Ravello.

One evening, Sandro D'Urso took us to a lovely house near Naples for dinner. Neapolitan cuisine has specialties like spaghetti or eggplant with chocolate sauce, but happily we didn't have either of these. On the table in the living room was a shotgun (it was apparently an old Neapolitan custom to keep a shotgun on the table). On arrival, one of our houseguests went over to pick it up and, not realizing it was loaded, fired it. The Secret Service rushed into the room. Everyone was paralyzed with fear.

These magical days drifted serenely from one to the next. Perhaps part of what made one enjoy them so deeply was knowing how special and carefree they were.

Conca — a fishing village on the
Amalfi Coast is my idea of paradise

# SOUTHAMPTON

*I* spent my early childhood in Easthampton, and the ocean has always been important to me. I longed for it during the many years I was in Europe.

When I returned from England and rented Andy Warhol's house, I realized I should get my own place and that it would be better for Anthony and Tina not to be isolated at the very end of Long Island.

Southampton was an hour closer to the city, and I'd heard there was a beach house that might be right for the three of us. It was perfection, with a deck jutting over the beach almost straight into the ocean. When you went to sleep, you felt you were at sea.

We spent twelve great years there.

Ocean days with my Golden Retrievers
Zack & Zoom

The living room of the beach house
with the floor looking like the ocean.

The deck, with the view on the beach.

# CHRISTMAS

*A*mong the many happy times in our house in England, Christmas was the most memorable. The tradition of giving a play for our mother every Christmas Eve had begun when we were very young. Jackie and I sang carols, while I played the Virgin Mary and she played Joseph. Later, we varied it a bit to the Three Kings and the shepherds. The final carol we sang was always "One Night, When Stars Were Shining," which touched my mother so much that she was always reduced to tears. No one else seems ever to have heard of this carol, but it was her favorite.

One Christmas at Turville, we presented Anthony and Tina with an old gypsy caravan which they believed the gypsies had left for them during the night. They invited us in for tea parties with all the dogs.

Wherever we were, whether Turville or Palm Beach, with Jackie and Jack, Caroline and John, Anthony and Tina, these traditions continued. The Christmas Eve play was the most important event

24

With Stas, Christmas at Turville.

of the holiday. For days in advance, the children busied themselves rehearsing their roles and designing their costumes. Caroline usually played the Virgin Mary, Tina was an angel and the boys were the Three Kings. Small as they were, there were heated discussions and much excitement over the costumes, which were mainly colorful scarves and fake jewelry from our bureau drawers, interspersed with Christmas tree decorations.

In between carols, the children would sometimes switch to being reindeers in harness—"Dancer," "Prancer," "Cupid" and "Vixen." We tried to have our children repeat the particular carol I used to sing with Jackie, but with little success. Then everyone hung their stockings, left Santa something to eat, and prayed with excitement until dawn.

The other big event of the holiday was the Wrightsman's New Year's Eve party. It was always the most beautiful evening and you knew from the moment you walked into their orchid-filled house that everything was going to be perfect and delicious. About seventy people would attend, including all the President's family, his sisters and brothers-in-law, Eunice and Sarge Shriver, Pat and Peter Lawford, Jean and Steve Smith, the President's mother, Rose Kennedy, Vice President Lyndon Johnson, when he was visiting, and the Secretary of Defense Robert McNamara. It was elegant, yet very festive.

*(Preceding pages)* Christmas at Turville (1969).

*(Opposite)* Anthony and Caroline.

*(Following pages)* Christmas in Palm Beach (1961).

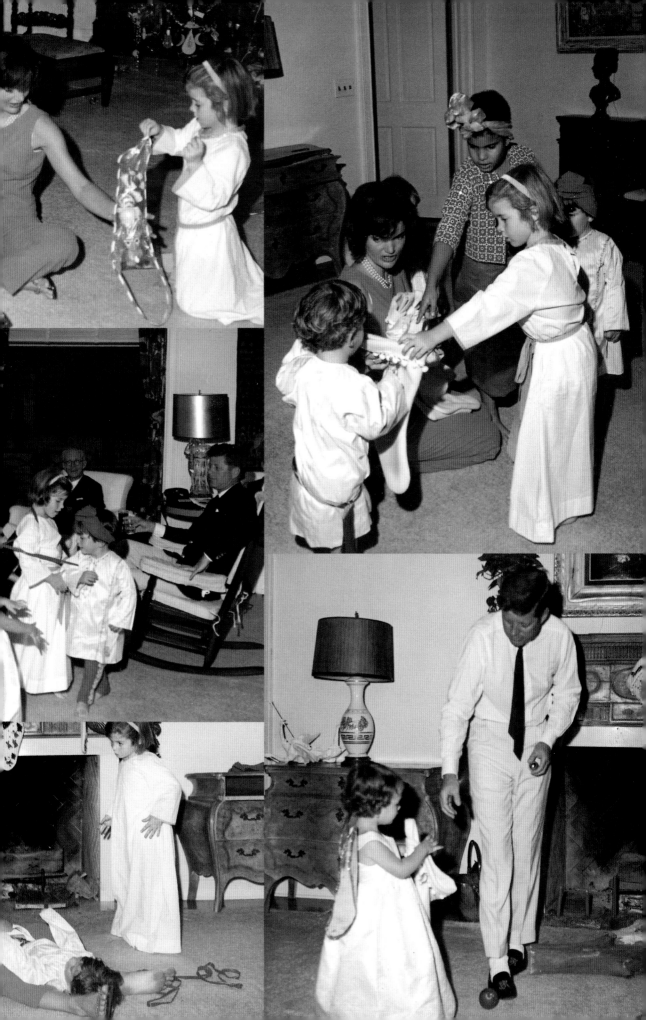

# MONTAUK, ANDY AND THE BEALES

*T*first met Andy Warhol when I returned from London and wanted to rent a house by the sea on Long Island. He had just bought an extraordinary place on Montauk Point. It was a fishing camp designed in the late twenties by Stanford White so the owner, a certain Mr. Church, could visit in the late summer with his friends, who stayed in small lodges built around the main house. It was called "Eoönen" (dawn). The main house had a floor of huge old flagstones and two enormous fireplaces opposite each other. It smelled of cedar and the sea.

Andy came by the apartment to meet me. He was accompanied by a large entourage, including Paul Morrissey, Fred Hughes, Bob Collacello and Vincent Fremont. Everyone was silent for a while, but finally the reason for the gathering was raised, and it was agreed that I would rent the house, although it hadn't been lived in for many years. We had wonderful times there, with many birthday celebrations for Anthony and Tina, and Andy. I gave him an enormous flagpole

At Montauk, by Andy Warhol.

to stand between the house and the sea. It was a great addition, and we had the flag flying every day.

Although Andy was always very quiet and mainly said "Gee whiz," you always knew he was taking everything in, sharp as a computer. He was dressed perpetually in jeans, was close to painfully thin and wore his trademark wig. The wig and "Gee whiz" were the first things that came to mind when you thought of Andy.

He was almost allergic to fresh air, but once in a while felt obliged to leave the city and check in on the happenings at his place in Montauk. Here a somewhat different person was on display. He loved children and was inventive with them, creating activities in which they became totally absorbed, such as when he sat them down at a large round table in the living room to show them how to edit film in a simple way. He was something of a pied piper, always keeping their attention, always admiring and encouraging them at whatever they did.

We spent long lazy afternoons on the beach, talking and burying each other in the sand. At times like this, Andy wasn't as strange as he initially seemed, but revealed himself as a keen, subtle observer of everything around him.

He had a simple supper every night at six before going out, seven nights a week, to observe. He couldn't eat the rich food at the dinners and parties that he constantly attended. He was too fragile after the attempt on his life and his serious operation.

Andy had a sharp sense of business and a vision which has since been proved to be extraordinary—whether it was in real estate, Polaroids, or cookie jars.

Often, Truman Capote drove over from Bridgehampton to lunch and gossip for the rest of the day, and Peter Beard was forever doing his collages, moving a windmill from Montauk to the cliffs near the point, inventing something of interest for Anthony and Tina. Watergate was on the television non-stop and that was consuming.

Soon we were making a film of my childhood in Easthampton, using my Aunt Edith Beale as the narrator, and so a large part of our days on Long Island were spent in Easthampton, at "Grey Gardens," the home of Aunt Edie and her daughter, "Little Edie." Peter had suggested the Maysle brothers would be the perfect filmmakers for this project—they had just received accolades for their documentary on Altamont, the notorious Rolling Stones' concert and they used a 16-mm camera, which the Beales would find less threatening.

It took over a month for me to persuade Aunt Edie that she could trust the Maysles and that she would actually enjoy this project, which indeed she and "Little Edie" did. They couldn't get enough of the camera, talking and in particular sparring with one another. "Little Edie" had not left the town of Easthampton for twenty-five years, so her views on the outside world were based mainly on her imagination.

The smell of their sixty cats in the house was something I could never get used to. Nevertheless, some very trying times were matched with amusing ones, mother and daughter giving us some hilarious and theatrical shows of love and hatred, mixed with highly original observations.

Some days I brought a picnic, and we would invite the intelligent and civilized priest of Most Holy Trinity Church, Father Huntington, to join us. These were peaceful interludes from the constant bickering between mother and daughter.

The Maysles became so intrigued by the project that they persuaded me to let them control it completely, making it a film solely on mother and daughter. *Grey Gardens* is a cult film today.

"Andy Warhol's *Interview*," 1975.

Andy Warhol's
Interview

Mar
25¢

Many Happy
Returns
of the day
Aug 5-6, 1972
A.W. B-day from F.

Mrs Winters

The flagpole, my birthday present to Andy.

INTERVIEW: Do you have any big regrets, Lee?

LR: Well, my deep regret is that I wasn't brought up or educated to have a *métier*.

I think if you see a spark of interest in a child or young person you should immediately make an effort to expose them as much as possible to that particular field.

The only thing that gives you any real sense of fulfillment is to accomplish something, no matter how small or insignificant it might be considered. I think so many people can't bear to be alone with themselves.

INTERVIEW: What kind of person do you admire, Lee?

LR: That's difficult to say, but offhand, I admire people who have self-discipline, determination and compassion.

INTERVIEW: You've passed through a lot of different stages in your life—do you have an "ultimate ambition?"

LR: I have passed through the stages of ambition and I think the most serene feeling is to know you are being true to yourself. I also think it's rewarding when you're satisfied with something you've accomplished and look forward to something else ahead.

Apart from that, to be at peace with yourself, to have largesse and curiosity and see your children happy in what they're involved in, if they're fortunate enough to want to be involved in something of interest.

It all sounds so easy, but we can see that it isn't.

INTERVIEW: Do you feel that you're a complete New Yorker now Lee?

LR: Enormously, because I've always known this city terribly well, and I wouldn't want to

With Andy.

With Mick and Bianca Jagger, in Montauk.

live anywhere else in the world. But it does seem as if New York is basically a city to sell one's wares and then vanish. The majority are out hustling and that's depressing, but it adds to the intensity of the atmosphere. We're too success orientated which is fooling since success is so ephemeral. Here today, gone tomorrow. You can never have any good friends or relationships if you are only fascinated by success. It's too short to thrive on.

You could say New York is a merciless city, but if you are able to retreat, which I find essential, you can happily cope with it.

INTERVIEW: So you're a city girl? But when I see you in the country you really look like a country girl.

LR: You see me always looking like a wet rat emerging from the sea. Contrasts are great, aren't they? It makes you appreciate everything so much more. When you're at the sea you love returning back to New York. If you're fortunate enough to be able to have a couple of contrasts. I mean to get out for weekends alone, to walk the beach or the country in order to keep your peace of mind.

And New York changes physically so much. Each year it's so fascinating because it's changed so much. Everything you're attached to has been torn down and everything looks so different. But the great thing about New York is that there's no moment of the year when it's asleep, whether it's broiling-hot August or what.

(Extracted from *LEE* by Andy Warhol)
*Interview*, Sunday, February 2, 1975, 1:00 P.M.

Beach games in Montauk

Andy with Dick Cavitt.

Vincent
Fremont

Andy Warhol

an

# PALM BEACH

*W*e especially looked forward to leaving the gray rainy days of London for Palm Beach at Christmas. Jack and Jackie were lent a large house on the ocean, very near Jack's family house. We were excited about being together.

Anthony and Tina would play on the beach with Caroline and John, and Jackie and I would spend hours talking every day and being with the children. It was wonderful to be together again. Stas played backgammon with Jack, who also occasionally played a round of golf, depending on the condition of his back. The White House staff would stay nearby, and would come and go during the day as Jack needed them, but the atmosphere was very pleasant and relaxed.

When the weather was fine, we would spend the day on the presidential yacht, the *Honey Fitz*, named after the President's grandfather, John Francis Fitzgerald, the famous mayor of Boston. The Secret Service would follow behind in several smaller boats.

Before we arrived in Palm Beach, Jack had read that the majority

Anthony and Caroline in Palm Beach.

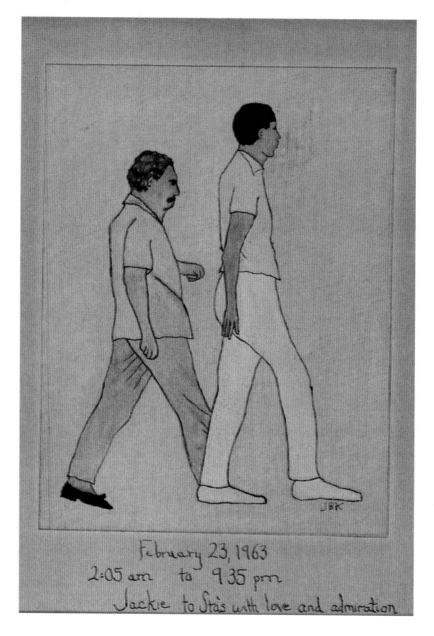

February 23, 1963
2:05 am to 9:35 pm
Jackie to Stás with love and admiration

Stas and Chuck's fifty-mile walk, by Jackie, February 23, 1963.

*(Opposite)*
Stas and Oleg Cassini, February 1963.
*(Following pages)*
"En route" to lunch on the *Honey Fitz,*
the presidential yacht, named after the President's grandfather
"Honey" Fitzgerald, the famous mayor of Boston.
The President and his brothers-in-law, Stephen Smith and Stas.

of Americans were not fit enough to walk fifty miles. This concerned him and, discussing it with Stas and his good friend Charles "Chuck" Spalding, who was visiting,

he challenged them to do a fifty-mile walk, never dreaming they could possibly make it.

They accepted the challenge and bets from many members of the family, as long as they would be given two months to get into shape. A date was fixed for late February, over Washington's birthday weekend, when we would all be returning to Palm Beach. The stipulation from the President was that the walk would have to be completed within twenty hours. It was completed in nineteen and a half.

Stas and Chuck were about as different physically as any two human beings could be. Stas was far shorter and stockier. Chuck was extremely tall and thin. Stas had never done any exercise in his life, not even walking, while Chuck had played a little golf. Neither had much stamina. Nevertheless, they strongly believed they could do it and took up the challenge. Every day for two months Stas would practice in New York with a stopwatch, walking fifty blocks up and down Park Avenue, with a look of fierce determination on his face and a stone in each hand to keep his fingers from swelling.

It was decided that because of the heat, the walk should start in the early hours of the morning. Setting off at 2:05 A.M., they walked on the side of the highway, from Palm Beach to Fort Worth, exactly fifty miles. It was a flat, straight stretch, so they could be watched closely.

Jackie and I were following in a station wagon, with supplies for their resuscitation. Chuck wanted to snack on raw meat, while Stas wanted only orange juice. Their physical types were as different as their tastes.

When they were close to exhaustion, they would collapse briefly on the side of the road, time was of the essence. Triumphantly, they met their challenge, won their bets and walked into Fort Worth a half hour early.

Jackie did a watercolor for Stas to commemorate his feat.

Lunch at sea on the *Honey Fitz*.

# TRUMAN CAPOTE

$\mathcal{I}$ don't know where or when I first met

Truman Capote. Like several people close to me,

I hear his voice often as if we were together now.

We had great times together, and he was a big influence.

He had this extraordinary gift of being a confidant. A great raconteur,

he loved to entertain and was about the best company one could ever

have. He could also be very generous, and sensitive to other people's

needs. Truman encouraged me to go on the stage and perform publicly

for the first time in my life. He thought the role of Tracy in Philip Barry's

*The Philadelphia Story* was ideal for me. Of course, following

in Katherine Hepburn's footsteps was awesome to say the least,

but I loved the theater and was willing to take my chances and

Truman's constant encouragement reassured me.

I asked Yves Saint Laurent to design the costumes—which he did,

beautifully. I will always remember the very heavy white crepe dressing

With Truman at his Black and White Ball.

gown he designed for Tracy when she was carried to her room by Dexter, somewhat the worse for wear.

At the last moment, Truman insisted I have a great make-up artist, so George Masters flew in from Hollywood. Truman made it sound as if everything depended on it, so I agreed.

The play opened in Chicago. It began with Tracy writing a letter at her desk. I felt paralyzed and my hand couldn't cross the page. After what seemed an eternity, I managed to write one word repeatedly, and so overcame my anxiety.

On opening night, the press was out of control. I felt some reviews had been written in advance, but I never had any regrets. I liked my fellow actors and learned a great deal from the whole experience. I found particularly interesting the extent to which the audiences differed. Matinée audiences were always the best, because they were determined to enjoy themselves.

Later, Truman devoted much time and energy to planning his Black and White Ball in New York. It was in honor of Katharine Graham, who was head of the Washington Post Company and had been widowed recently.

People talked about the ball for months in advance—what kind of mask would they wear; whom would they order their black or white dress from; whose dinner would they attend; who was or wasn't invited. My spiral silver sequin dress was made by Mila Schön, who came from Milan to London several times for fittings, as well as to oversee the mask.

There was much expectation in the air. We went first to the Paleys for dinner and then on to the Grand Ballroom of the Plaza Hotel, where the spectacular ball was held. The elegance of the room was incomparable. The orchestra was impossible not to dance to and everyone was at his best, full of expectation and ready to have a wonderful time. Lauren Bacall waltzed with Jerome Robbins and cleared the floor.

Stas and I left with Truman and Henry Ford at 5:00 A.M. and went to have breakfast at *The Brasserie* on Park Avenue. We were so elated, and wished it wasn't all over.

One year, shortly after Christmas, I went to visit Truman at his Palm Springs house. I arrived wearing a new sable coat, which had been a present from Stas. We went out to the movies that night, and when we returned and I went to my room, I could hardly believe what I saw. Charlie, Truman's bulldog, was lying on what remained of my coat, which was shredded in small pieces around him. I'll never forget Truman's uncontrollable laughter in the face of this disaster. For him, everything provided a pretext to laugh.

*Leaving the theater*

Daintly wiping his mouth ... about fashion. "I don't think women look good in p... an can wear them. I usually tell women if I don't like them in pants, what do like are those fake Fortuny dresses. The fakes are more amusing than the real ones. Gloria Guinness has lots. Babe has plenty too. She's never out of them, so I don't know when she has time to wear all those Halstons."

Although Truman hasn't published a book since "In Cold Blood" in 1966, he says he feels no pressures. "The work I put in it has to move at its own pace. It has to move like a river. Yes, I have control. I can speed things up, but I actually only work four hours a day." Truman starts giggling again to himself. "You see, I waste two hours getting ready to start and then I take a big, long nap. By that time it's an eight-hour day! Writing is like cooking. You get nauseated, but you have to keep on. I get sick to death of my cooking sometimes, but I got to keep on cooking."

In October of 1969, Truman told a WWD reporter he was two-thirds away from finishing his book "Answered Prayers." Today Truman says, "I'm two-thirds away from finishing the book. I've spent nearly all my life on this book. It's very long. I had the notes and the construction made and then 'In Cold Blood' came up. I never dreamed it would take so long to write.

"It's about answered prayers. There are more tears shed over answered prayers than unanswered ones. That's the worst thing that could happen to you, to have all your prayers answered." About his own prayers, Truman is mum.

He is more talkative about the "The Great Gatsby" film script controversy which rose after Truman was assigned to write it by Paramount. "They wanted me to do it. I like the book but I thought it would be difficult to make a film out of it. Everything that happens, happens off stage or two years before. Everyone told me I shouldn't do it, but I went ahead and

stars."

The meal finished, Truman re-w... photographer. He pays the check ... LeSabre. "I had to borrow this one... a forest green Buick. I got so sick a... parts."

Truman jams down his rumple... "It's my favorite hat, but I don't r...

He throws the car into gear an... Southampton. There's a brief sto... Paul Simon's new record."

It is Truman's idea to be phot... the exquisite grounds of pal Kay ... like a Bertolucci film. Let's ca... son,'" giggles Truman putting ... honey blond doghairs down the l... the vacant pool. "This is the sa... Fosburgh did of me that the Me...

The shooting finally winds u... erative. "I never read anythin... ther." Truman removes his c... "I'm going home to have a li... and read a book." And with a... Sagaponack calling over his s... of the story won't you?"

Truman in the *Rolling Stones Magazine*.

Lee, my dreamer or Truman

ON THE BRINK: Less
days after the Pre
calling for the

The Cliff

With Truman in Montauk.

# Lee

## a fan letter from Truman Capote

Ah, the Princess!

Well, she's easily described.

She's a beauty. Inside. Outside.

What I like about her best is that she can be both cozy and candid at the same time, a very rare combination, an almost impossible one; still, if you ask her opinion, be prepared for an honest reply—honest, yet always delivered in a manner that is warm and encouraging.

Yet, she is reticent, she never forces advice upon you—she waits until you ask, or until she sees you really need it. That of course is part of her first-class intelligence and part of her femininity—which brings us to another interesting and singular combination of qualities in her character: I can't think of any woman *more* feminine than Lee Radziwill—not even Audrey Hepburn or a great seductress like Gloria Guinness—yet she is not at all effeminate. She *reacts* like a remarkably resilient young man: nothing fazes her—not really; also, she is a mover, she *moves,* she's a delicate but durable athlete, a water creature, an Ondine: to watch her swimming in Caribbean waters, or to see her sweeping on water skis across the sea's horizon, is the most excellent experience.

It's odd about eyes; all the greatest artists I've known had remarkable eyes: Colette, Camus, Isak Dinesen, Willa Cather (the faded blue of autumnal Nebraska skies), Garbo, Brando, Chaplin, Proust (of course, I never knew him, but one can tell from the photographs), Tennessee Williams (so brimming with fag merriment), Carson McCullers, Billie Holiday, Jane Bowles—gosh, one could go on for several pages, but what is generally true about gifted people, is even truer about women of classical beauty and substance: it is impossible for a woman to be classically beautiful unless she has beautiful eyes, or can create the illusion that she does. Lee does—wide-apart, gold-brown like a glass of brandy resting on a table in front of firelight, and it is with those eyes that she recognizes the qualities of a room, a person sitting in it, and the very happenings in his heart.

Extracted from *Vogue,* June 1976.

The opening of *The Philadelphia Story.*

The Black and White Ball:
Marella Agnelli, Christiana Brandolini, Brando Brandolini,
David Beaufort, Cecil Beaton and I.

# "EXTREME MAGIC"

rives careening to and fro. "May I have an egg, please?"

Lee says: "Oh, Luciana. How *can* you?"

At dusk this day the sea calmed as the "Tritona" approached the stony Montenegro coast. Everyone, feeling vastly better, is on deck staring down at the green-crystal depths skidding below. Suddenly a trio of sailors, standing in the ship's prow, start to shout and gesture: An immense porpoise is racing along beside us.

The porpoise leaps, arcs, gleefully descends out of sight, leaps like laughter materialized, plunges again, and this time disappears. Then the sailors, leaning over the rail, begin to whistle a curious intense whistle-chant, and the whistling is some Ondine melody.

Extracted from *Vogue*, April 15th, 1967.

On the Agnelli's boat:
with Gianni Agnelli
and Carlo Caracciolo.

# LONDON

$B$uckingham Place is a very small street in London, parallel to Buckingham Palace. When Stas and I first moved in, there was a vast brewery nearby, with horse-drawn carriages loaded with kegs of beer. Picturesque as it was, the smell was not so nice. A few years later, it changed, replaced by office buildings that dominated our little street of lovely eighteenth-century houses. It was a dramatic contrast.

Living in London in the sixties was full of excitement. There was a renaissance in every aspect of culture. From music to fashion, the arts were flourishing, and everything was changing with incredible speed. The National Theatre, where I went several times a week, was at its peak, with Olivier, Gielgud and Ralph Richardson performing regularly. The Royal Ballet had a rebirth, due to Nureyev's new partnership with Fonteyn.

Antique shops opened all over London, and auction houses had more and more great sales, which I often attended and where I learned

With Thomas.

most of what I know now. London was bursting with life.

In 1959, I had married Stas Radziwill in a civil ceremony at Merry Wood, the house of my mother and stepfather outside of Washington. He was a remarkable figure with an enormous heart, a particular sense of humor and a great knowledge of history. My mother's indignant remark when I introduced him to her—"Why, he is nothing but a European version of your father!"—made me love him all the more! Stas was twenty years older than me, and I learned more from him than I have ever learned from anyone else. We had two children, and although they were only a year apart in age, Anthony and Tina were completely different. Anthony loved sports and animals; Tina was passionate about ballet and the arts.

In June of 1960, Tina was christened in London at Westminster Abbey. President Kennedy was her godfather.

Returning from a trip to Paris, where we met General de Gaulle, Jack and Jackie came to London to stay with us at Buckingham Place. The fact that Tina had survived—she was born three months prematurely—made it an extraordinary event and her christening was an occasion for particular celebration. Jack, realizing this, made a great effort to be there following

Tina and Anthony by Cecil Beaton.

his meetings with Khrushchev in Vienna and de Gaulle in Paris.

While we were in Paris, the Secret Service had arrived at Buckingham Place and had turned the house inside out—to the point that the press was able to sneak in under the guise of being moving men, taking photographs of the entire house. This was upsetting, but in England all the media was fascinated by this unusual end to the President's trip.

After the christening ceremony, where the godmother was Stas' sister, Christina Potocka, we went back to our house where we had a small reception for friends and people Jack particularly wanted to see.

That night we went to Buckingham Palace for a small, informal dinner, since the President's visit was not official. I remember thinking the place mats depicting scenes of London were strangely quaint. The Queen gave us a tour of the Picture Galleries. She was impressively knowledgeable and had a great deal to say about the history of each painting.

My days in London were never routine. Some were spent watching Nureyev rehearse or take a class, others were spent at events at the Lycée Français, where both Anthony and Tina went to school. We traveled a lot—sometimes to Kenya, which Stas adored.

John, Anthony and Tina watching the Changing of the Guard at Buckingham Palace (1966).

I met a number of extraordinary artists who became friends. Leonard
Bernstein was one of them. I remember when he visited us in London
and invited me to the rehearsals for his recording of Mahler's symphonies.
As the *Second Symphony* was being televised, it was performed in the evening with
thousands of candles in St. Paul's Cathedral. The chorus in that magnificent space
was overpowering.

Lennie was a man of great passion and charisma, as was Rudolf Nureyev,
who had a unique magnetism and whose insatiable curiosity about everything—
whether intellectual, artistic or political—made him endlessly fascinating.
His physical strength was awesome.

Rudolf came to live with us for six months. His schedule was quite different
from ours. He woke up in the afternoon, having slept under a sea of blankets
in order to make him sweat. The bed was drenched. He used to order a blue
steak for lunch at around 3:00 or 4:00 P.M. and never returned home until well
after midnight.

After a performance, in order to wind down, he loved to walk by all
the antique shops he knew to see if there was anything he longed for.
There usually was, and inevitably someone from his entourage would be sent out
the next day to buy it.

I spent the weekend with him just after he bought his first house, "La Turbie,"
in Monaco. It was like a Greek church, all white stucco and iron grill gates dividing
the rooms. Baroque music was always playing. It was the first of his many future
homes in London, Paris, New York and Virginia—all of them dramatic.

Another of my close friends was Cecil Beaton. We often had lunch at
one another's house and he would describe his portrait sittings with

the Queen and the Queen Mother (always with palms in the background), or his work in Hollywood for the film *My Fair Lady* with Audrey Hepburn, or his theater designs. He was a particularly good raconteur, with great wit and a strong sense of the mischievous. He had the most amusing drawl and inflections and loved to pose, somewhat coyly, with an arched head.

Cecil never believed in his talent; in fact, he would often say that he had none. But I had the greatest admiration for his discipline. At every opportunity, when he wasn't working, he was taking a daily class at the Royal Academy of Arts, always eager to improve himself.

His house in Wiltshire was full of charm, straight from an Oscar Wilde set. The mauve dining room, which was lined with palms, led into a slightly failing winter garden, whereas his house in London was very smart, with black lacquer walls and gold silk in the sitting room. But then Cecil loved to change things frequently, depending on his work at the time.

*Jackie & Antony*

*Tina's Grad Parents*

*Top left:* Tina's christening.
*Top right:* with Cecil Beaton, at the opening of *Coco.*
*Bottom left:* Rudolf Nureyev, Anthony and I in Turville.

*Middle right:* Anthony in the living room
*Bottom right:* a corner in Buckingham Pl

*Opposite:* the godparents at Tina's christening, Westminster Abbey, London.

# TURVILLE

*T*urville was a seventeenth-century Queen Anne bakehouse outside of Henley-on-Thames, Oxfordshire. It was unpretentious, but a lovely property. The brick façade faced Turville Heath, while the gardens and the back overlooked the Chiltern Valley.

It was roughly fifty acres, part of which we turned into a miniature village by laying out a cobblestone courtyard adjacent to the main house. The courtyard was surrounded by a large guesthouse, a small stable with a dovecote above, and an herb garden. In the middle was a big beech tree surrounded by an octagonal bench for mounting horses. There was a large kitchen garden and a rose garden behind with pink walls and espaliered pear trees lining the paths. It was a dream.

There was a tennis court in the fields nearby where Noel Coward-like tennis was occasionally played.

Stas was responsible for the indoor pool, which was a brief walk from the house in a low brick building with a lead roof in the middle of the orchard. It was very dramatic inside.

We went every weekend, as well as holidays, and spent part of the summer there. It was only an hour drive from London, so many visiting friends came out for lunch and spent the day, and the guesthouse was always full for weekends.

There were a lot of animals, although I never could have too many. In all, we had one cat, Pussy Willow, five dogs, three horses and a pony. I can't imagine life without dogs and have always had one. It was a constant pleasure to ride my beautiful horse, Topaz, through the valley and the lovely countryside beyond.

Turville was a house of flowers. When you entered, it had a smell of straw rugs and burning fires mixed with the scent of sweet flowers. Each room was covered with them, whether it was the silk panels of the living room, picked out and bordered in the colors of Cantonese enamel with pale green and pink flowers, or the dining room, strewn with them painted over Sicilian scarves on the walls.

Outside the living room, there was a huge catalpa tree which I wanted to frame, so with great difficulty we created an "œil-de-bœuf" window over the fireplace in order to see it.

There was much croquet and a lot of gardening. The large English garden led into a double alley of chestnut trees overlooking the Chiltern Valley and fields of sheep beyond. It was very French in feeling, with moss covering the ground and a large old stone urn placed on a pillar in the center just before the ha-ha. In the spring, it was covered with thousands of bluebells and daffodils.

Although we went to the sea every summer so our children could be together, when they were at Turville time had a very Chekhovian rhythm, reminding me of A *Month in the Country.*

The dining room in Turville.

The Gypsy Caravan

The Cobblestone Courtyard

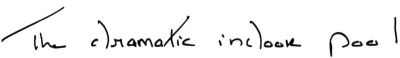

The dramatic indoor pool

Ari telling Tina's fortune

My Bedroom

The room between the living room and the library
was a room of birds where Pedro, the parrot,
and Samba, the toucan, hung in large brass cages.

# FIFTH AVENUE

*J*ackie moved to New York in 1964, and Robert Kennedy persuaded Stas, who hated the city, to buy an apartment there, so I could be near her at least part of the year. Stas didn't like the idea at all, and no one except Bobby could possibly have talked him into it.

I found the perfect apartment, at 969 Fifth Avenue, and made it into a place I loved. Soon the children were in school there.

Although I had two of the prettiest houses in England, I wanted my children to feel closer to New York and to their cousins, and I wanted to be near Jackie and spend more time there. It was where I was happiest. The rhythm was different then. Life was more gentle. Everyone had more time to relax, appreciate looking at things and visit museums. It was normal to lunch at people's apartments rather than in a restaurant; and some, like Pamela Harriman, always made it feel like a special occasion in a warm and welcoming atmosphere with several guests. In those days, nobody would dream of asking for water

Portrait by René Bouché.

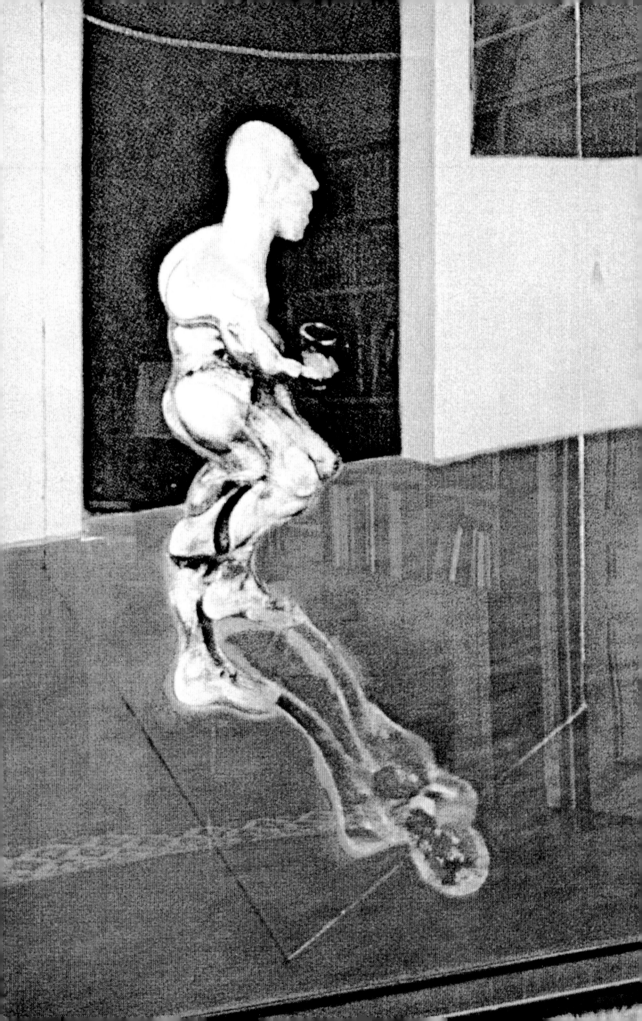

In the library,
with Francis Bacon's
*Man in a Cage.*

The living room
Fifth Avenue

before a meal! Of course, there were glamorous restaurants like *The Colony,* where Diana Vreeland always had her table and would swoosh in to greet everyone, always in black, occasionally with a dash of red, and command a vodka "strait." No one ever left before 3:00 P.M.

The apartment was a duplex overlooking the trees of Central Park and the pale green leaded roof of what is now the New York University of Fine Arts. As it was in a very dilapidated state, we gutted it completely. I asked Renzo Mongiardino to imagine the living room, and he chose a beautiful cherry-red velvet, which he stenciled very subtly and surrounded with red, black lacquer and gilt frames. The curtains were lettuce green taffeta with a border of woven colored velvet to tie in with the large Bessarabian rug.

My favorite paintings, a series of boar hunting in India by James Ward, hung around the room. They were too decorative to look bloodthirsty, and I loved them, having methodically acquired them separately at auction over a period of years. In the hall-library hung a Francis Bacon of a man in a cage, which Stas had acquired by paying Francis' gambling debts. Jackie gave me beautifully bound sets of Balzac and Voltaire. Dark orange moiré covered the dining room walls, with a particularly amusing painting of a monkey shaking hands with a dog. I wanted my bedroom to resemble a greenhouse as much as possible, with a pale green and white color scheme which gave it a very airy feeling. I filled it with large ferns and hung Anglo-Indian botanical watercolors on the walls. When I woke up, it felt like I was in the country.

Anthony and Tina went to school in New York before Anthony went off to boarding school at Choate and Tina remained home to go to Brearley.

When the children were older, I moved to a smaller apartment. It was a charming penthouse on Park Avenue, which had an entirely different feeling, even though it was only two blocks away. It was more like Turville, in that all the fabrics on the wall were strewn with flowers, giving it a country feel, with French doors opening onto the terrace. I used most of the same furniture, so it had an echo of the past. It was lovely, but I missed Anthony and Tina a lot.

My menu book

Page 96: in the Fifth Avenue dining room, with a "nursery" eighteenth-century painting of a monkey shaking hands with a dog.
Page 97: in front of the James Ward painting Boar Hunting in India.

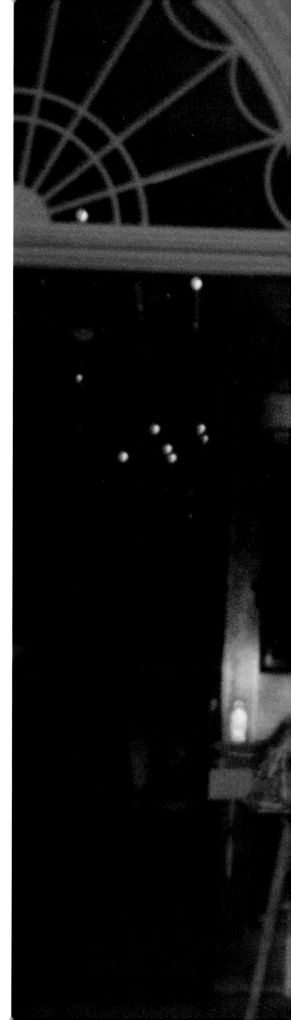

With Lenny Bernstein
at The White House

The Penthouse — Park Avenue

With Nehru.

Lord Lambton with
Prime Minister
Harold MacMillan.

Stas and Oleg Cassini.

A banquet in Pakistan.

Anthony's first day.

A painting of Jackie
and I playing chess.

Chiquita Astor

Rome.

de Versailles,
w York.

In the Wrightsman's
swimming pool, Palm Beach

Thomas.

Jamaica, 1959.

Jackie hugging Stas on our return from India.

Anthony with Thomas.

The President's car returning home from Tina's christening.

Anthony with Tina.

At the Elysée Palace.

# INDIA

It was almost blinding as we stepped off the plane in New Delhi into a galaxy of colors. Prime Minister Nehru was at the bottom of the ramp encircled by women in brilliant saris—a sea of pink, fuchsia, turquoise and yellow against the most brilliant blue sky.

We left in a motorcade with Nehru, his daughter Indira Gandhi (the future Prime Minister) and our beloved ambassador, John Kenneth Galbraith, who was with his wife, Kitty. The road was lined with hundreds of thousands of people, many of them children who had shown up to welcome Jackie. There were triumphal arches saying "Long Live Mrs. Kennedy," including one from the wine merchants of New Delhi which was really a surprise in that country.

After we arrived at Nehru's house, we went for a walk in the Mogul Gardens, which were exactly like all the Indian miniatures one had ever seen. We then went to the Rajghat to lay roses for Gandhi, and toured hospitals, orphanages and the local craft centers.

With Jackie in New Delhi.

From New Delhi we took the President's train, which previously had belonged to the viceroys, to visit Fatehpur Sikri, a sixteenth-century city of red sandstone encircling the palaces of the queens, and passed through Agra to see the Taj Mahal. The crowds were tremendous and the press was nearly out of control. My first glimpse of what is perhaps the greatest tribute ever to love will always remain indelibly imprinted in my mind. Its outline against the sky is as fine as an ink-drawn line.

Of all the places we saw, Udaipur remains the most memorable because it seemed so unreal. The Maharana, a very attractive man, was our host. He took us on a tour of the island, with Jackie's enormous entourage of Indian officials and princes, and many journalists and cameramen in tow. It was a lovely scene, somewhat like a regatta, with children shouting "Welcome to the American Maharani."

Our last stop on this unforgettable trip was a visit to Jaipur, and my good friends the Maharajah and Maharani of Jaipur, Jai and Ayesha. Thousands of children and young Rajastani girls dressed in vivid colors lined the route, dancing and singing to welcome Jackie.

The Jaipurs, whom we stayed with, had arranged many festivities, but most outstanding was the drive to Amber, a twelfth-century city in the Rajput Hills, where we found several magnificent elephants waiting for us to take a ride. There were so many hundreds of cameramen, I was surprised they didn't frighten the elephants, but their behavior was impeccable. It was a colorful moment, but all too brief.

The next morning, the Galbraiths and Nehru came to the airport to see us off. We were so sorry to leave. It had been an extraordinary visit, and I will always remember Nehru as the most fascinating, gentle and sensual man I ever met.

With Ambassador John Kenneth Galbraith and his wife Kitty.

With Jackie at the Amber Palace.

*Afternoon Tea*, by Jacqueline Duhême.

In the receiving line in Udaipur Palace.

Watching Rajahstani dancing

Mrs. Kennedy
Goes Abroad

JACQUELINE DUHÈME
INTRODUCTION BY JOHN KENNETH GALBRAITH
TEXT BY VIBHUTI PATEL

ARTISAN
in association with Callaway
New York

In President Ayub Khan's gardens

A banquet in Pakistan

Jackie with Nehru.

# GREECE

In the summer of 1971, I went with my children to the island of Skorpios. I had been sick and Jackie thought it would help me recuperate.

It was a beautiful part of the world, covered with almond and lemon trees, set in a satin sea, with a magnificent coastline. I felt better and stronger every day in a lovely little pink house on the saddle of the island overlooking the Ionian Sea, surrounded by olive trees. The terrace was the center of a life spent talking, painting and making collages. These were perfect days.

Most of August was silent with heat.

We used to spend much of our time at the Beach House. Sometimes, we would take out the caïque named *Caroline* for a delicious picnic lunch with the children.

In the late afternoon, when the heat had subsided, we would take a bottle of rosé and water-ski for hours, or sail with Aristotle Onassis to Lefcos on the mainland for an ouzo in the harbor. Ari was always greeted

With Caroline and Tina in Mykonos.

by the men of the island, who stopped by to pay their respects and exchange local news. For him, life was a chess game and it had to be played that way. Once he had made his winning move, the game was over. His patience was enduring; time was unimportant. In fact, he seemed to have no concept of time at all.

Ari was magnetic. He walked like a potentate, noticing and wanting to be noticed. He enjoyed observing, with an habitual cigar in his hand. His hair was thick with brilliantine and his olive skin was smooth. His voice sounded like soft gravel—raspy, but low. He was usually saturated with eau de cologne when he was dressed in his heavy silk shirts and ready to leave for Athens in his seaplane.

In order to bring some diversity to the evenings, we would have special festivities for birthdays, such as the one for Jackie's, on July 28th, where Anthony and John, dressed as two musketeers jousting in a fencing match, played an unforgettable *Cyrano de Bergerac* for us.

The caïque *Caroline,* Skorpios.

*(Following pages)*
Summer in Skorpios by Peter Beard.

KODAK SAFE

→12       →12A       → 11       →11A       → 10

KODAK SAFETY FILM

→18       →18A       →17       →17A       →16

KODAK TRI X P

→24       H   K   C       →23       →23A       →22

Carefree Summer Days

KODAK TRI X PAN FILM

→29       →29A       →28

On the Caïque Caroline

Having a drink in Delfici

At the beach house

Tina

With Prime Minister & Mrs Karamanlis at the theater — Epidaurus

# MY SISTER

One always looks up to older siblings for guidance. One tries to emulate them, and follow their achievements. That's what I did with my sister.

But as we were so different physically, Jackie being strong and athletic, I being soft and chubby, I never followed her when she rode horses, in spite of my father's efforts.

JVB, my father, was special. The Black Prince, or the Black Orchid as he was also known, had enormous style and charm, which set him apart from the rest. If a word must be conjured up to describe him, it is "dashing"—which is what he was, in every sense of the word. We adored him. To be with him when we were children meant joy, excitement and love. He brought gaiety to everything we did together, and he encouraged us to enter wholeheartedly into the things we loved. For Jackie, it was her passion for horses and riding. For me, it was the sea.

With Jackie and Tina outside the White House.

Jackie and Lee 1935

He taught me to trust the sea and to share his love for it. I can still hear him calling out to us, "Come on! Swim out to the last barrel! Now get under those waves, so you won't get somersaulted and torn to pieces! Here comes a beauty—ride this one in! Hold my hand, hang on to my shoulders. Let's go!" Being with my father during those early summers, having him to ourselves for days on end, was a joy.

Sometimes I've been asked if I felt that my father favored Jackie. Of course he did. That was very clear to me, but I didn't resent it, because I understood he had reason to. First of all, he'd been with her for four years before I was born, and those first years are very binding. Second, he wanted a son more than anything, so she was not only named after him—or at least as close as you could get a girl's name to a boy's—but she actually looked almost exactly like him, which was a source of great pride to my father.

But if I didn't come in for as much praise as Jackie, I also didn't receive the same amount of criticism as she did. He was so vulnerable to any imagined slight or neglect on her part, that reproach upon reproach was directed at my sister.

In letter after letter, he told us that he wanted us to excel, to be superior, to be the best. He wrote to Jackie when she was a student at Miss Porter's school in Farmington:

> I do so, Jackie, want you to be a standout at school. In fact, I've such high ambitions for you, I know you've got it in you to be a leader. But what's more, I know "you've got what it takes" to make your schoolmates like and admire you. I'd be terribly happy if some fine day you were voted to have done most for your school, and became the most respected. That has much more to it than being the most popular. However, I'm not worried about you; I know you have it in you. Just make it come out and show them . . .

Her performance at school was uppermost in his mind, and he wrote frequent letters of encouragement:

> Do hard work, don't waste your time, but take advantage of all opportunities to get ahead, whether it be in your studies or in little daily lessons that confront you each day. You know I'm proud of you. Always keep me that way, never let me down, and always remember in your own heart that I will never let you down. I miss you and love you a great deal.

My mother labeled us, and often said to friends, "Jacqueline is the intellectual one, and Lee will have twelve children and live in a rose-covered cottage." Of course, I kept this in mind, but in my case it certainly did not turn out to be true.

In spite of our different interests, Jackie and I were extremely close and shared the emotional difficulties of children with divorced parents. I looked up to her, counted on her and admired her. Although we occasionally fought fiercely, that came to an end when I finally triumphed by pushing her down the stairs. From that moment on, she realized I could stand up to her, and the childhood fights were over.

Jackie was a reader, an excellent student who had great intellectual curiosity matched with a sense of mischief and humor. Since I was four years younger, I felt no urge to compete, and lived more in an imaginary world centered on friends and activities such as painting and modeling with clay.

When Jackie went off to boarding school, I was very lonely and missed her terribly. We wrote one another constantly, and her letters had much more news than mine since I was alone in a very large house with none of the activities boarding school life provides. The dogs and horses were my main companions, as my mother and stepfather were often away. I missed Jackie so much that I even thought about adopting an orphan!

A costume class
Easthampton

In Central Park

Winning the

leadline class

Jackie with Caroline, John, Anthony and Tina in Turville.

Finally, I too went to Miss Porter's school, in Farmington, Connecticut. But it was the year after Jackie had left, and I had to face the inevitable comparisons from mutual teachers. In the end, I didn't like it half as much as she did.

The greatest gift to me while I was there was having an extraordinary art history teacher, Sarah McLennan, who changed my world with her passion for the subject. I lived for her class, and started corresponding with the art historian Bernard Berenson, who had a considerable influence on me. I began to categorize things under his favorite terms, "life enhancing" or "life diminishing." We finally met at his famous villa, I Tatti, in Florence when I went to Europe for the first time with Jackie.

One of the most painful experiences we had to go through was having boys call for us at JVB's apartment to take us out to holiday dances. I remember feeling sick with nerves when one of these miserable young men was ushered into my father's presence and subjected to close scrutiny and cross-examination. Just the thought of the questions he would ask filled me with apprehension

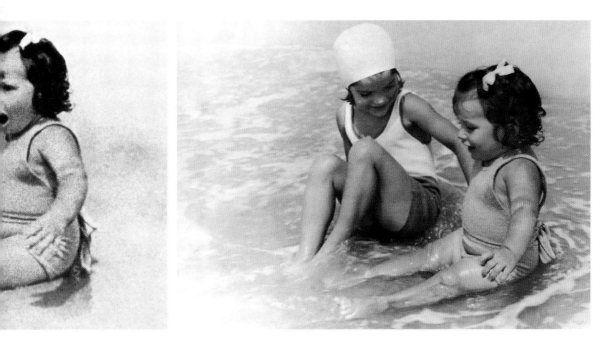

Easthampton, circa 1935.

and terror: "Please don't ask him what college he intends to go to!" (everyone had to go to father's alma mater, Yale). "Or what secret society he belongs to!" (Skull & Bones, the most powerful, was his). "Who cares if his family isn't in the Social Register!"

I doubt whether my father ever felt in his heart that any man was good enough for either of his daughters. But he managed to convince himself that John Kennedy would be a really good husband for his beloved daughter—in spite of the fact that his future son-in-law had gone to Harvard instead of Yale, and in spite of the fact that Joseph P. Kennedy had worked for President Roosevelt on the Securities and Exchange Commission, which JVB felt had ruined him financially. Surprisingly, they had a great deal in common—especially humor—and both took a passionate interest in sports.

With the wedding, Jackie's destiny led to another life. As the wife of the President of the United States, she was extremely busy. She had to travel a lot and liked to have me with her, as we were very close. Apart from great mutual affection, I think our strongest bond was a shared sense of humor, which was endlessly enjoyable. From the several trips the two of us made to India, Pakistan, Greece, Morocco or France, I should mention an example of my sister's typically mischievous humor. In 1962, we went on a private visit to Morocco, where we were the guests of King Hassan and his sisters for several extraordinary days. The King had renovated the Bahia Palace in Marrakech for our visit. After our arrival in Marrakech, we were brought to meet him at one of his palaces, where not only his harem lived but also the harem of his late father as well as his grandfather.

We were told that the King had been delayed by urgent news, so one hour passed, and then another. Jackie and I had difficulty keeping the conversation going with almost one hundred smiling and giggling ladies dressed in golden caftans in the middle of a magnificent courtyard. After a second hour had passed, Jackie rose to her feet and announced that her sister, who had a beautiful voice, would now get up and sing for them our mother's two favorite songs from childhood: "In An Old Dutch Garden Where The Tulips Grow," followed by "The White Cliffs of Dover."

I was in disbelief to see how amused Jackie was by the situation she'd put me in. The entire harem was delighted, oohing and ahing with joy and anticipation over the performance they were about to witness. There was no way out. I got on my feet and began . . . I was only pleased to amuse so many people, especially my sister who was in hysterical laughter.

On the terrace at Conca, by Benno Graziani (summer 1962).

# ONE
# SPECIAL SUMMER

Cover of the book *One Special Summer*, 1974.
*The following pages are extracted from the book.*

I, the undersigned, Secretary of State
of the United States of America, hereby
request all whom it may concern to per-
mit safely and freely to pass, and in case
of need to give all lawful aid and protec-
tion to.

JACQUELINE LEE BOUVIER
a citizen of the United States.
The bearer is accompanied by his
Wife, XXX
Minor children XXX
         XXX
         XXX

Given under my
hand and the
seal of the
Department of
State
at Washington
MAY 27TH
19 48

Nº 218793

Passport

United States of America     27
Department of State

tion to
CAROLINE LEE BOUVIER
a citizen of the United States
The bearer is accompanied by his
Wife, XXX
Minor Children, XXX
         XXX
         XXX

Given under my
hand and the
seal of the
Department of
State
at Washington
MARCH 21ST
19 51

United States of America
Department of State

At 9:45 pm, June 7, 1951, after pleading and pestering and praying for a
year— Nº 218793 and Nº 545527 left the country.

# ONE

# SPECIAL

# SUMMER

Written and Illustrated
by
Jacqueline and Lee Bouvier

YES THANK YOU,

WE HAD A

LOVELY CROSSING

The other "girl" sharing our cabin was 99 year old Miss Coones. She frightened me enough with her clothes on, but when she turned on the light about 4 am for the 6th consecutive time I threw back my bed curtain and was horrified to see Miss Coones' bony naked body - After that I decided I didn't WANT to know what was going on in that cabin. Telegrams arrived for us between 6 and 7 am and Miss Coones would stand by the door shouting "For JackLyn" — "For Lee". Today we were terribly lucky and managed to get switched to a cabin by ourselves. A trip with Miss Coones would have been a fascinating experience, but a little exhausting.

On the 3rd class deck today we met Fausi Shehadi who is about 35 or 40 - from Lebanon - and very much resembles Ali Khan. It's like having a flirtatious puppy around and we simply send him off to do all our errands. However I do think he has deeper motives and Jackie has warned me about the quirks in the sex lives of Near Easterners!!

Last night Jackie and I tried to make ourselves look respectable to sneak into 1st Class. We tore across the 3rd class deck, lept over a large fence, whizzed down 1 flight of stairs, lept over another fence — and finally we were there. I keep catching my heel in the hem of my dress which wastes a lot of time. I'm sure I'll have broken every bone in my body by the time we arrive. We spend most of the time dodging officers and now have the guilt expressions on our faces whenever one looks at us. I have this fear that soon we'll be caught in the act — the whistles will blow — the ship will ha while we are condemned.

**3RD CLASS** PLEASE OBSERVE SOCIAL BARRIERS

MASTER AT ARMS

Cables arriving steadily every day all day long — and in turn they're goin out steadily which means our money is rapidly vanishing in vast sums It started with a cable from Mr. Bevan saying:

DINNER DANCE ARRANGED LONDON WEDNESDAY EVENING VERY MUCH LOOKING
FORWARD SEEING YOU CALL FOR DETAILS CAMBRIDGE 4410 ON ARRIVAL
                                                        BEVAN

Last night after dinner I felt I simply had to dance and informed Jackie I was about to pick someone up, when suddenly a form of humanity appeared before me known as Iganovich Illiwitz from Persia, and whisked me around the dance floor. The only thing I could see in the whole room was his nose — and then he kept trying to proudly point out his family to me. I finally realized which they were — It was the same nose on the same face of everyone of them, only it came in all sizes. Suddenly I noticed Jackie waltzing around with the purser who I had dreamt of all day. I was absolutely infuriated by this and simply repulsed everytime I had to look at Iganovich.

This afternoon a fat old woman was seasick in the same bathroom I was in, and two of her front teeth were lost in the event. She wanted me to help her find them in the last disposal, but she had apparently flushed them down the toilet with her first deposit. That really made me feel on top of the world for the rest of the day.

"Aw just sing her something from "Call Me Madam.""

IV

But once we got on to it — it took us all over the place —

"Excuse me — Can you tell me what country this is?"

V

Until we sold it in Paris

Spanish diplomats and schoolteachers and a Yugoslavian with his 6 Mafia friends who wanted to give us the money in a shoebox, and a G.I. who we hid the dent from by parking it against a wall, came to peer and poke at it, while we stood by trying to look nonchalant. We finally sold it to Harrison Davidson Esq. who said he was a missionary but looked as if he had just escaped from Benny Goodmans String Quartet. He was going to take it to the Sahara Desert and wanted it cheap because $5. could keep an African child alive for a month and every $5. he spent on himself meant one more would starve to death. We were for slaughtering the whole tribe but his conscience would only let him starve 206 of them.

I must tell you about Chamber Music at Mrs. Johnson's. It was the most agonizing experience of my life. Mrs J. told us Pleven and Bevan were coming and we were to arrive at 10:30. "Oh good", said Jackie, "That means the concert and a fabulous souper afterwards." All week we had been in a state about what to wear. At the last minute I asked the maid to take in my white lace dress which she did by clutching two great handfuls and sewing them up. It was so tight Jackie had to wear it. She could only get into it sideways so she looked rather strange from the front. We had no dinner and spent the evening in a frenzy of getting ready. As we clumped out the door, me in a great yellow thing of Jackies I kept tripping on, I moaned "Oh I dont even want to go." "Dont you ever want to meet fascinating people or just spend all your time with your dreary little American friends", exploded Jackie as we raced down the hall.

We stumbled up the stairs of 34 Rue de la Faisanderie after a harrowing taxi ride. Jackie had had a wad of money ready ever since Place de la Concorde. A fabulous souper my foot — They were all in the dining room still eating dinner! While 10 or 12 butlers were busily lighting chandeliers we tiptoed around the room too terrified to even smoke because we might dirty a Louis XVI ashtray.

Finally with a great roar the dining room doors burst open and they came towards us— a horde of Ambassadors, Dukes, Counts and Princes, and women with emerald necklaces clanging against their knees. They would only speak to someone if they were a notch above them so you can imagine how many spoke to us. We trotted around behind Mrs J. as she introduced us – "and here I have two Bouviers", to people who sneered at us over their shoulders. Suddenly, as I was introduced to the Indian Ambassador all wound up in turbans, I felt every article of underclothing fall to my feet. I was panic struck and couldn't decide which was best — to walk away leaving them in the middle of the room pretending I knew nothing about them — or to gracefully stoop and pick them all up underneath my skirt. Somehow I managed not to let it be seen, and spent the rest of the evening hopping like a toad, clasping my ankles.

As we were standing behind the Indian Ambassador — I didn't dare move very far — up came my one friend, this hearty creature called Mrs MacArthur — always roaring and slapping her thigh. She slapped me and a Frenchwoman on the back and said:

"Hey, get that character, will you —" pointing to a priceless Ribera of St. Peter over the mantle, "he looks just like the Indian Ambassador they stuck me next to at dinner." I shrieked with nervous hysteria until I caught Mrs Johnson's beady eye.

The Chamber Music began. Half the room obviously knew nothing about it but would have died rather than admit it. They all put on these enraptured facial expressions — Mrs J. looked as if she was undergoing some sweet agony — forehead wrinkled slightly, nostrils dilated and a sad smile. A woman near me was beating time — rocking back and forth in her chair in such ecstasy that I was afraid she would lurch into my lap. After each squeaky little piece they all outdid themselves to think up a new adjective of praise. Jackie and I were sitting in the hall with two furious Counts. I started to smoke and one of them handed me a fat gold walnut for an ashtray. It got so hot it was like clutching a live coal. Finally I could stand it no longer and gave it back to him to put on the table. You could smell burning flesh as he took it. He let out a curse "Merde," and dropped it on the floor where it rolled spilling ashes. Everyone whirled on him in horrified indignation, hissing Ssshhh — He really loved me after that.

After the music was over they passed champagne and strawberry cakes that were too big to get in your mouth in one bite and too runny to keep in your hand — and then it was time to go.

Paul de Ganay was doing his military service at Poitiers and we had promised to stop and see him on our way to Spain.

We cruised aimlessly around the town pleading out the window "S'il vous plaît, ou est le 3ème Régiment 8ème Escadron des Dragons?" A truckload of cheering soldiers side-swiped us, shouting "Suivez-nous"! We were off — over rutted dirt roads, swerving as they backfired in our faces and cried "Qu'elle conduit bien, la petite!"

We drew up to a dirty yellow caserne. There was a row of soldiers on either side of the gate and someone marching down the middle. We drove gaily in and asked if anyone would possibly know where we could find l'Aspirant de Ganay. They weren't too cordial. It turned out some general was pinning on medals and we had chugged right up the middle of his guard of honor.

We fled. Someone had told us Paul's Escadron was doing Manoeuvres on a field out of town. We heard guns booming in the distance and followed our ears across uncharted regions of bumpy pasture. Through smoke and dust clouds we could distinguish foxholes. We jumped out at each one, ran belly to the ground through No Man's Land to peer in and inquire if anyone knew where we could possibly find l'Aspirant de Ganay. Leering French faces looked up at us blankly. Invitations to climb down and join them were offered freely, but no clues to Paul.

A fruitless hour landed us in a cross-fire of flame belching anti-tank guns. A clump of trees was the only haven in sight. I rolled up the windows to deflect shrapnel, crouched on the floor of the car and yelled "Come on here — You can make it if you really try!" We careened into the clump and screeched to a stop at the feet of the 2 best looking officers this side of Paradise. They wore blue berets and had lovely gold cords twining underneath their arms. We tumbled out, patting our hair into place and inquired if anyone knew where we could possibly find l'Aspirant de Ganay. The Lieutenant smiled. I had to put on my sunglasses to intercept the ardor of his glance. He blew a whistle and 3 minutes later, trotting through the trees came the object of our Search.

"Paul!" we cried, and sprang for him. He recoiled and greeted us very formally. We were crushed. It would have been such fun to kiss him on both cheeks the way they do in news-reels. He stood there, a ramrod of agony and disapproval while we toed the ground nervously, wishing we had sweaters to cover up our strapless sun-dresses.

Then the Lieutenant stepped forward and saluted Paul. "Elles sont sensationnelles, vos amies, de Ganay" he rolled in the tones of the Order Of The Day. "Vous êtes fiancé?" "Oui mon Lieutenant, avec les deux", Paul saluted back.

Another knee-weakening smile from the Lieutenant informed us we could take Paul away. He got in the car, we zoomed up the motor and were off into the anti-tank fire, the Marseillaise throbbing in our heads and thanking God for the North Atlantic Treaty.

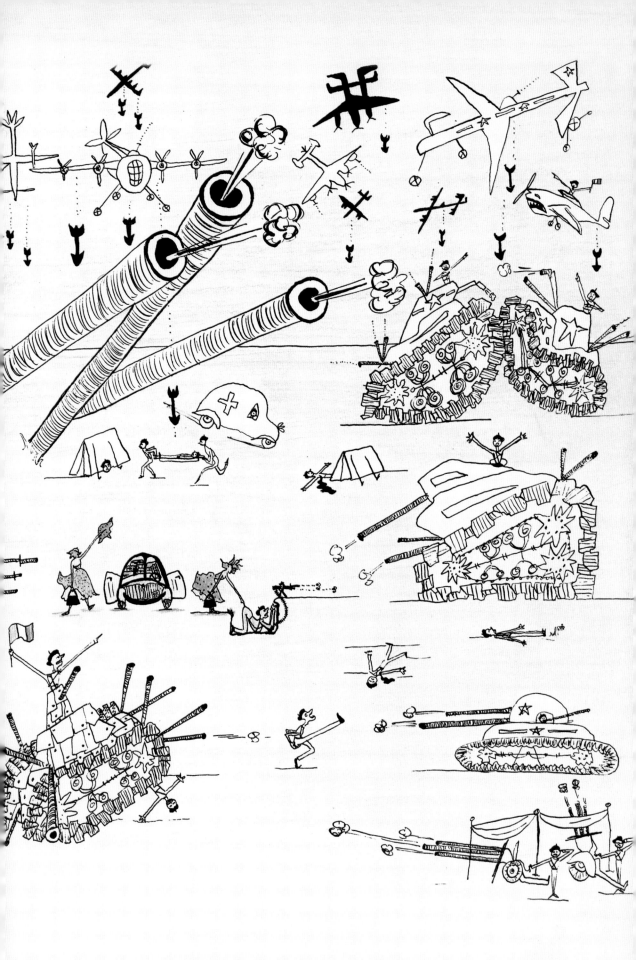

Jackie so plump and full of attraction
Posed for Fazzini and came out abstraction

we put his statue of a stalking cat in the courtyard and took pictures of the real cats
hissing at it... He couldn't speak English - nor we Italian but we talked together incessantly
Such a gentle vie de Boheme - no bearded Paris cynics - When we left for Naples in our
groaning car - they all came out into the pink street and waved goodbye -

Christian and Alfonso Hohenlohe took us out to El Quexigal — their house that had been a monastery in the time of Phillip II. We sat in Columbus' chair — tiptoed around tables full of crown jewels — gaped at pictures signed Love George V and just felt we should be taking notes for History of Art 105 but all they wanted to do was make Ma and Pa change the vic while we jitterbugged to "Wave the Green For Old Tulane" underneath the Flemish Primitives.

# PHOTO CREDITS

*All photographs belong to Lee Radziwill's private collection except:*

*First cover and second flap*: © Bettmann/Corbis — *First flap, Pages* 38 (*left*), 40 (*bottom*)-43, 62-63,122-124,166-167(*bottom left, bottom right*): © Peter Beard — *Pages* 17, 59, 167 (*middle top*): © Pierre Boulat/Life/Pix —*Pages* 19, 23: © Photograph by Harry Benson, 1977 — *Pages* 20-22: © Jaime Ardiles-Arce/*Architectural Digest*/The Condé-Nast Publications Ltd. — *Pages* 25-27: © Benno Graziani — *Page* 33 *and back cover*: © Andy Warhol/Adagp, Paris 2001 — *Pages* 36-37: © Bill King/*Interview Magazine*, "Andy Warhol's interview," 1975 — *Pages* 57, 64-65: © Life/Pix — *Pages* 68-69: © Marella Agnelli/*Vogue*/The Condé-Nast Publications Ltd. — *Page* 71: © Henry Clarke/ *Vogue's New Beauty Book*/The Condé-Nast Publications Ltd. — *Pages* 72-73: © Cecil Beaton/ Sotheby's Picture Library — *Pages* 78-79, 114,116 (*middle; top and bottom right*): © Jacqueline Duhême/*Mrs. Kennedy Goes Abroad*, Artisan, New York — *Pages* 80 (*middle and bottom right*), 96-99,105: © Richard Champion / *Architectural Digest*/The Condé-Nast Publications Ltd. — *Pages* 85-87, 89-91: © Horst/ *Vogue*/The Condé-Nast Publications Ltd. — *Page* 91: © René Bouché, 1958 — *Pages* 94-95: © The Condé-Nast Publications Ltd./*Man in a Cage*, Francis Bacon, Adagp, Paris 2001 — *Page* 104: © Derry Moore/ *Architectural Digest*/The Condé-Nast Publications Ltd. — *Page* 143: © Ron Galella/Corbis Sygma — *Pages* 146-165: © *One Special Summer*, by Jacqueline and Lee Bouvier, Eleanor Friede, Delacorbe Press, New York.

# ACKNOWLEDGMENTS

I particularly want to thank Martine Assouline for her steadfastness, encouragement and friendship since we first met, and Prosper Assouline for his great eye and immense charm. My special thanks to Andrew Wylie, who I've always counted on.
This book would not have been possible without the generosity of my great friends Benno Graziani and Peter Beard, and the help of Charlie Scheips, Harry Benson, Bill King and Janet McClelland, Michael Stier (*Vogue* Archives, U.S.), Lucy Watson (*Vogue*, Great Britain), Juliet Hacking (The Beaton Archive), Anne Mahe (*Life*/Pix), Françoise Carminati (Corbis Sygma) and Véronique Guarrigue (Adagp, Paris).
Also my thanks to Mathilde Dupuy d'Angeac, Véronique Billiotte, Laurence Stasi, Bernard Wooding, Aurore de la Bretesche and Bertrand Doisnel for their efficiency and follow through.